Official Rules of
Tennis

This book is available in quantity at special discounts for your group or organization. For further information, contact:

Triumph Books
542 South Dearborn Street
Suite 750
Chicago, Illinois 60605
(312) 939-3330
Fax (312) 663-3557

Printed in U.S.A.

ISBN 978-1-60078-552-8

This cover and design treatment copyright © Triumph Books
Cover design by Patricia Frey
Cover photo courtesy of AP/Wide World Images
Interior design by Sue Knopf

Contents

User's Guide

This edition of the *Official Rules of Tennis* has been designed to give tennis fans of all ages a quick and easy reference guide to the action on the court.

This edition contains the following material, in the format indicated:

The Rules of Tennis, as drafted by the International Tennis Federation, of which the United States Tennis Association is a member.

USTA Comments
These sections provide the reader with supplementary information intended to help clarify the rules. The United States Tennis Association drafts these comments.

*ITF **Notes** provide additional information to the section of the rule being referenced. The International Tennis Federation drafts these notes.*

EXPLANATORY NOTE

The following Rules of Tennis and Cases and Decisions are the official rules of the International Tennis Federation (ITF), of which the United States Tennis Association (USTA) is a member. USTA Comments have the same weight and force in USTA tournaments as do ITF Cases and Decisions.

When a match is played without officials, The Code shall apply in any situation not covered by the ITF Rules of Tennis.

Except where otherwise stated, every reference in the ITF Rules of Tennis to the masculine includes the feminine gender.

Where substantive changes have been made since the last edition of the ITF Rules of Tennis, there is a vertical line in the margin.

Reference to the International Tennis Federation or ITF shall hereinafter mean ITF Limited.

The
Rules of
Tennis

1. THE COURT

The court shall be a rectangle, 78 feet (23.77 m) long and, for singles matches, 27 feet (8.23 m) wide. For doubles matches, the court shall be 36 feet (10.97 m) wide.

The court shall be divided across the middle by a net suspended by a cord or metal cable which shall pass over or be attached to two net posts at a height of 3½ feet (1.07 m). The net shall be fully extended so that it completely fills the space between the two net posts and it must be of sufficiently small mesh to ensure that a ball cannot pass through it. The height of the net shall be 3 feet (0.914 m) at the centre, where it shall be held down tightly by a strap. A band shall cover the cord or metal cable and the top of the net. The strap and band shall be completely white.

- The maximum diameter of the cord or metal cable shall be ⅓ inch (0.8 cm).

- The maximum width of the strap shall be 2 inches (5 cm).

- The band shall be between 2 inches (5 cm) and 2½ inches (6.35 cm) deep on each side.

For doubles matches, the centres of the net posts shall be 3 feet (0.914 m) outside the doubles court on each side.

For singles matches, if a singles net is used, the centres of the net posts shall be 3 feet (0.914 m) outside the singles court on each side. If a doubles net is used, then the net shall be supported, at a height of 3½ feet (1.07 m), by two singles sticks, the centres of which shall be 3 feet (0.914 m) outside the singles court on each side.

- The net posts shall not be more than 6 inches (15 cm) square or 6 inches (15 cm) in diameter.

- The singles sticks shall not be more than 3 inches (7.5 cm) square or 3 inches (7.5 cm) in diameter.

- The net posts and singles sticks shall not be more than 1 inch (2.5 cm) above the top of the net cord.

The lines at the ends of the court are called baselines and the lines at the sides of the court are called sidelines.

Two lines shall be drawn between the singles sidelines, 21 feet (6.40 m) from each side of the net, parallel with the net. These lines are called the servicelines. On each side of the net, the area between the serviceline and the net shall be divided into two equal parts, the service courts, by the centre serviceline. The centre serviceline shall be drawn parallel with the singles sidelines and half way between them.

Each baseline shall be divided in half by a centre mark, 4 inches (10 cm) in length, which shall be drawn inside the court and parallel with the singles sidelines.

- The centre service line and centre mark shall be 2 inches (5 cm) wide.

- The other lines of the court shall be between 1 inch (2.5 cm) and 2 inches (5 cm) wide, except that the baselines may be up to 4 inches (10 cm) wide.

All court measurements shall be made to the outside of the lines and all lines of the court shall be of the same colour clearly contrasting with the colour of the surface.

No advertising is allowed on the court, net, strap, band, net posts or singles sticks except as provided in Appendix III.

In addition to the court described above, the court designated as "red" and the court designated as "orange" in Appendix VI can be used for 10 and under tennis competition.

USTA Comment 1.1
How do you tighten the net to the proper tension? First, loosen the center strap. Next, tighten the net cord until the center of the net is approximately 40 inches above the ground. Finally, tighten the center strap until the center of the net is 36 inches above the ground. These measurements should always be made before the day's first match and when possible before each match.

USTA Comment 1.2
What happens if a singles stick falls to the court during a point? The point stops immediately and is replayed.

USTA Comment 1.3
A regular 78-foot court with permanent QuickStart Tennis format lines is suitable for sanctioned play in divisions that require a 78- foot court.

2. PERMANENT FIXTURES

The permanent fixtures of the court include the backstops and sidestops, the spectators, the stands and seats for spectators, all other fixtures around and above the court, the Chair Umpire, Line Umpires, Net Umpire and ball persons when in their recognised positions.

In a singles match played with a doubles net and singles sticks, the net posts and the part of the net outside the singles sticks are permanent fixtures and are not considered as net posts or part of the net.

3. THE BALL

Balls, which are approved for play under the Rules of Tennis, must comply with the specifications in Appendix I.

From January 2012, for 10 and under tennis competition the balls described in Appendix I cannot be used. Instead one of the stage 3 (red), stage 2 (orange), or stage 1 (green) balls described in Appendix VI must be used.

The International Tennis Federation shall rule on the question of whether any ball or prototype complies with Appendix I or is otherwise approved, or not approved, for play. Such ruling may be taken on its own initiative, or upon application by any party with a bona fide interest therein, including any player, equipment manufacturer or National Association or members thereof. Such rulings and applications shall be made in accordance with the applicable Review and Hearing Procedures of the International Tennis Federation (see Appendix VII).

The event organisers must announce in advance of the event:

a.   The number of balls for play (2, 3, 4 or 6).

b.   The ball change policy, if any.

Ball changes, if any, can be made either:

i. After an agreed odd number of games, in which case, the first ball change in the match shall take place two games earlier than for the rest of the match, to make allowance for the warm-up. A tie-break game counts as one game for the ball change. A ball change shall not take place at the beginning of a tie-break game. In this case, the ball change shall be delayed until the beginning of the second game of the next set; or

ii. At the beginning of a set

If a ball gets broken during play, the point shall be replayed.

Case 1: If a ball is soft at the end of a point, should the point be replayed?

Decision: If the ball is soft, not broken, the point shall not be replayed.

Note: Any ball to be used in a tournament which is played under the Rules of Tennis, must be named on the official ITF list of approved balls issued by the International Tennis Federation.

USTA Comment 3.1
What is the difference between a broken ball and a soft ball? A broken ball has no compression; a soft ball has some compression. Both broken and soft balls should be removed from play.

USTA Comment 3.2
May a player cause a ball to become wet by using the ball to wipe perspiration from the player's body? No. A player may not take any action that materially changes the condition of the ball; therefore, a player may not use a ball to wipe off perspiration.

USTA Comment 3.3
A current list of USTA approved balls is available on the USTA web site, www.usta. com.

---

4. THE RACKET

Rackets, which are approved for play under the Rules of Tennis, must comply with the specifications in Appendix II.

The International Tennis Federation shall rule on the question of whether any racket or prototype complies with Appendix II or is otherwise approved, or not approved, for play. Such ruling may be undertaken on its own initiative, or upon application by any party with a bona fide interest therein, including any player, equipment manufacturer or National Association or members thereof. Such rulings and applications shall be made in accordance with the applicable Review and Hearing Procedures of the International Tennis Federation (see Appendix VII).

> **Case 1:** Is more than one set of strings allowed on the hitting surface of a racket?
>
> **Decision:** No. The rule mentions a pattern (not patterns) of crossed strings. (See Appendix II.)
>
> **Case 2:** Is the stringing pattern of a racket considered to be generally uniform and flat if the strings are on more than one plane?
>
> **Decision:** No.

Case 3: Can vibration damping devices be placed on the strings of a racket? If so, where can they be placed?

Decision: Yes, but these devices may only be placed outside the pattern of the crossed strings.

Case 4: During a point, a player accidentally breaks the strings. Can the player continue to play another point with this racket?

Decision: Yes, except where specifically prohibited by event organisers.

Case 5: Is a player allowed to use more than one racket at any time during play?

Decision: No.

Case 6: Can a battery that affects playing characteristics be incorporated into a racket?

Decision: No. A battery is prohibited because it is an energy source, as are solar cells and other similar devices.

USTA Comment 4.1

What happens if it is discovered after play has begun that a player has been using an illegal racket or an illegally strung racket? All points played stand. The player must find another racket before continuing play. A player is subject to code violations for delay under the Point Penalty System. If the discovery occurs after the match is over, the match still counts.

USTA Comment 4.2

May a player who breaks a racket or a string in a racket leave the court to get a replacement? A player who leaves the court to get a replacement is subject to code violations for delays under the Point Penalty System. Rule 29b permits a player "reasonable extra time" to leave the court only in those cases where "clothing, footwear, or necessary equipment (excluding racket) is broken or needs to be replaced."

---

5. SCORE IN A GAME

a. Standard game

A standard game is scored as follows with the server's score being called first:

No point   "Love"
First point   "15"
Second point "30"
Third point   "40"
Fourth point "Game"

except that if each player/team has won three points, the score is "Deuce". After "Deuce", the score is "Advantage" for the player/team who wins the next point. If that same player/team also wins the next point, that player/team wins the "Game"; if the opposing player/team wins the next point, the score is again "Deuce". A player/team needs to win two consecutive points immediately after "Deuce" to win the "Game".

---

b. **Tie-break game**

During a tie-break game, points are scored "Zero", "1", "2", "3", etc. The first player/team to win seven points wins the "Game" and "Set", provided there is a margin of two points over the opponent(s). If necessary, the tie-break game shall continue until this margin is achieved.

The player whose turn it is to serve shall serve the first point of the tie-break game. The following two points shall be served by the opponent(s) (in doubles, the player of the opposing team due to serve next). After this, each player/team shall serve alternately for two consecutive points until the end of the tie-break game (in doubles, the rotation of service within each team shall continue in the same order as during that set).

The player/team whose turn it was to serve first in the tie-break game shall be the receiver in the first game of the following set.

Additional approved alternative scoring methods can be found in Appendix IV.

USTA Comment 5.1

Numeric scoring, which consists of "zero," "one," "two," and "three," may be substituted for "Love," "15," "30," and "40" as long as the principle of winning four points by a margin of two is preserved. This is particularly appropriate for matches between new or young players or in which one player does not understand English. Hand signals may be used to show the score. This is a common practice with players who are hearing impaired. Numeric scoring may also be used when No-Ad scoring is authorized.

USTA Comment 5.2

The tiebreak game should not be confused with the 10-Point Match Tiebreak, which under certain circumstances may be played in lieu of the deciding final set. The 10-Point Match Tiebreak is described in Appendix IV.

USTA Comment 5.3

Is the server required to call the score at the beginning of each game and the point scores as the games go on in matches without officials? Yes. This is required by The Code § 31. After an official has cautioned a player to call out the score, the official may in a particularly egregious case treat subsequent violations as code violations for unsportsmanlike conduct.

USTA Comment 5.4

The server states that the score is 40-15; the receiver states that the score is 30-30. The players agree on who won every point except for the second point. What should they do? They should replay the second point from the advantage court. If the server wins the point, the score becomes 40-15; if the receiver wins the point, the score becomes 30-30. The next point is played from the deuce court.

USTA Comment 5.5

What happens in the same situation as USTA Comment 5.4 except that the disputed point is the third point? Everything is done the same except that the disputed point is played from the deuce court.

USTA Comment 5.6

The players agree that they have played six points in the game but disagree over the score because they do not agree on who won the second point. The receiver acknowledges that the server called the score after each point and that the receiver did not express disagreement with the score until now. What should happen? The score as announced by the server should prevail because the receiver did not object. Note, however, if the receiver denied hearing the score, then an official would have to be called to go through the normal 3-step process to settle the dispute.

USTA Comment 5.7
When do the players change ends during a tiebreak? Players change ends after every six points and at the end of the tiebreak. (See Rule 10.) They shall change ends during the tiebreak without a rest.

6. SCORE IN A SET

There are different methods of scoring in a set. The two main methods are the "advantage set" and the "tie-break set". Either method may be used provided that the one to be used is announced in advance of the event. If the "tie-break set" method is to be used, it must also be announced whether the final set will be played as a "tie-break set" or an "advantage set".

USTA Comment 6.1
USTA Regulation I.E.1.a. prohibits the playing of "advantage sets."

a. "Advantage Set"
     The first player/team to win six games wins that "set", provided there is a margin of two games over the opponent(s). If necessary, the set shall continue until this margin is achieved.

b. "Tie-break Set"

The first player/team to win six games wins that "set", provided there is a margin of two games over the opponent(s). If the score reaches six games all, a tie-break game shall be played.

Additional approved alternative scoring methods can be found in Appendix IV.

7. SCORE IN A MATCH

A match can be played to the best of 3 sets (a player/team needs to win 2 sets to win the match) or to the best of 5 sets (a player/team needs to win 3 sets to win the match).

Additional approved alternative scoring methods can be found in Appendix IV.

8. SERVER & RECEIVER

The players/teams shall stand on opposite sides of the net. The server is the player who puts the ball into play for the first point. The receiver is the player who is ready to return the ball served by the server.

Case 1: Is the receiver allowed to stand outside the lines of the court?

Decision: Yes. The receiver may take any position inside or outside the lines on the receiver's side of the net.

9. CHOICE OF ENDS & SERVICE

The choice of ends and the choice to be server or receiver in the first game shall be decided by toss before the warm-up starts. The player/team who wins the toss may choose:

   a. To be server or receiver in the first game of the match, in which case the opponent(s) shall choose the end of the court for the first game of the match; or

   b. The end of the court for the first game of the match, in which case the opponent(s) shall choose to be server or receiver for the first game of the match; or

   c. To require the opponent(s) to make one of the above choices.

   Case 1: Do both players/teams have the right to new choices if the warm-up is stopped and the players leave the court?

   Decision: Yes. The result of the original toss stands, but new choices may be made by both players/teams.

USTA Comment 9.1
When should the toss be made? The toss should be made before the warm-up so that the players can warm-up on the same end from which they play their first game.

---

10. CHANGE OF ENDS

The players shall change ends at the end of the first, third and every subsequent odd game of each set. The players shall also change ends at the end of each set unless the total

---

number of games in that set is even, in which case the players change ends at the end of the first game of the next set.

During a tie-break game, players shall change ends after every six points.

Additional approved alternative procedures can be found in Appendix IV.

USTA Comment 10.1
Do the players change ends after a 7-Point Tiebreak is played to decide a set? Yes.

USTA Comment 10.2
When do the players change ends during a tiebreak that uses the Coman Tiebreak Procedure? The Coman Tiebreak Procedure is identical to the regular procedure except that the players change ends after the first point, then after every four points, and at the conclusion of the tiebreak.

---

11. BALL IN PLAY

Unless a fault or a let is called, the ball is in play from the moment the server hits the ball, and remains in play until the point is decided.

USTA Comment 11.1
Is a point decided when a good shot has clearly passed a player, or when an apparently bad shot passes over the baseline or sideline? No. A ball is in play until it bounces twice or lands outside the court, hits a permanent fixture, or hits a player. A ball that becomes embedded in the net is out of play.

USTA Comment 11.2

Must an out call on a player's shot to the opponent's court be made before the opponent's return has either gone out of play or been hit by the first player? Yes.

12. BALL TOUCHES A LINE

If a ball touches a line, it is regarded as touching the court bounded by that line.

USTA Comment 12.1

If a player cannot call a ball out with certainty, should the player regard the ball as good? Yes. The Code § 6 and § 8 require a player to give the opponent the benefit of any doubt.

13. BALL TOUCHES A PERMANENT FIXTURE

If the ball in play touches a permanent fixture after it has hit the correct court, the player who hit the ball wins the point. If the ball in play touches a permanent fixture before it hits the ground, the player who hit the ball loses the point.

USTA Comment 13.1

What happens if a ball hits the top of the net outside the singles stick and then lands in the court? The player who hit the ball loses the point because the ball hit a permanent fixture. In singles the area outside the singles stick is a permanent fixture.

USTA Comment 13.2

Who wins the point if a player hits a ball that hits an object attached to the net or post (such as the scoring device) and then lands in the proper court? The player who hit the ball loses the point because it hit a permanent fixture before landing in the court.

USTA Comment 13.3

During a rally in a singles match played on a doubles court without singles sticks, a player hits a shot that was going out until it hits the doubles post and careens into the proper court. Who wins the point? Every effort should be made to provide singles sticks for a match that is played on a doubles court so that this situation does not occur. If it does occur, the player who hit the shot wins the point because the entire doubles net and doubles posts are respectively the net and the net posts for this match.

14. ORDER OF SERVICE

At the end of each standard game, the receiver shall become the server and the server shall become the receiver for the next game.

In doubles, the team due to serve in the first game of each set shall decide which player shall serve for that game. Similarly, before the second game starts, their opponents shall decide which player shall serve for that game. The partner of the player who served in the first game shall serve in the third game and the partner of the player who served in the second game shall serve in the fourth game. This rotation shall continue until the end of the set.

USTA Comment 14.1

May a doubles team switch its serving order at the beginning of any set or the 10-Point Match Tiebreak? Yes. There is no requirement that any doubles team retain the same serving order for a new set or 10-Point Match Tiebreak.

15. ORDER OF RECEIVING IN DOUBLES

The team which is due to receive in the first game of a set shall decide which player shall receive the first point in the game. Similarly, before the second game starts, their opponents shall decide which player shall receive the first point of that game. The player who was the receiver's partner for the first point of the game shall receive the second point and this rotation shall continue until the end of the game and the set.

After the receiver has returned the ball, either player in a team can hit the ball.

> **Case 1:** Is one member of a doubles team allowed to play alone against the opponents?
>
> **Decision:** No.

USTA Comment 15.1

On the first point of a set or 10-Point Match Tiebreak may a doubles team position both players on the deuce side of the court? No. The spirit of the rule requires that each partner take a position in either the deuce or ad court and that only the player positioned in the deuce court return the serve.

USTA Comment 15.2
May a doubles team switch its receiving order at the beginning of any set or match tiebreak? Yes. There is no requirement that any doubles team retain the same receiving order for a new set or match tiebreak.

USTA Comment 15.3
Do the partners have to alternate making shots during a rally? No. In the course of making a shot, only one partner may hit the ball. If both of them hit the ball, either simultaneously or consecutively, it is an illegal return. Mere clashing of rackets does not make a return illegal unless it is clear that more than one racket touched the ball.

16. THE SERVICE

Immediately before starting the service motion, the server shall stand at rest with both feet behind (i.e. further from the net than) the baseline and within the imaginary extensions of the centre mark and the sideline.

The server shall then release the ball by hand in any direction and hit the ball with the racket before the ball hits the ground. The service motion is completed at the moment that the player's racket hits or misses the ball. A player who is able to use only one arm may use the racket for the release of the ball.

USTA Comment 16.1
May a player serve underhanded? Yes. There is no restriction in the rules on the kind of service motion that a server may use.

17. SERVING

When serving in a standard game, the server shall stand behind alternate halves of the court, starting from the right half of the court in every game.

In a tie-break game, the service shall be served from behind alternate halves of the court, with the first served from the right half of the court.

The service shall pass over the net and hit the service court diagonally opposite, before the receiver returns it.

USTA Comment 17.1
What happens if the receiver volleys the serve? The server wins the point unless the serve hit the net, in which case it is a let.

---

18. FOOT FAULT

During the service motion, the server shall not:

a. Change position by walking or running, although slight movements of the feet are permitted; or

b. Touch the baseline or the court with either foot; or

c. Touch the area outside the imaginary extension of the sideline with either foot; or

d. Touch the imaginary extension of the centre mark with either foot.

If the server breaks this rule it is a "Foot Fault".

Case 1: In a singles match, is the server allowed to serve standing behind the part of the baseline between the singles sideline and the doubles sideline?

Decision: No.

Case 2: Is the server allowed to have one or both feet off the ground?

Decision: Yes.

USTA Comment 18.1

Where may the server stand? In singles, the server may stand anywhere behind the baseline between the imaginary extensions of the inside edge of the center mark and the outside edge of the singles sideline. In doubles, the server may stand anywhere behind the baseline between the imaginary extensions of the inside edge of the center mark and the outside edge of the doubles sideline.

USTA Comment 18.2

What does the rule mean when it says that the server may "not change position by walking or running"? One key to understanding this rule is to realize that the server's feet must be at rest immediately before beginning to serve. The delivery of the service then begins with any arm or racket motion and ends when the racket contacts the ball (or misses the ball in attempt to strike it).

To define walking or running with precision is difficult. This rule is intended to prevent the server from taking advantage of the receiver by serving while "on the move" and requiring the receiver to guess the position from which the serve will be launched, and the rule should be enforced with that intent in mind.

- A server who takes more than one step with either foot after the "feet at rest" position described above is at risk for being called for a foot fault. The serve becomes a foot fault when, in the judgment of an experienced official, the server has materially changed position before or during any racket or arm motion.

- A server whose footwork changes significantly from one serve to the next is at risk for being called for a foot fault.
- Serves that look like the running volleyball serve violate the rule. Serves in which the server runs or walks from a point well behind the baseline to the baseline are also illegal, as are serves in which the server walks or runs along the baseline before choosing a spot from which to deliver the serve.

USTA Comment 18.3

When does a foot fault occur? A player commits a foot fault if after the player's feet are at rest but before the player strikes the ball, either foot touches:

- the court, including the baseline;
- any part of the imaginary extension of the center mark; or
- beyond the imaginary extension of the outside of the singles sideline in singles or the doubles sideline in doubles.

USTA Comment 18.4

Is it a foot fault if the server's foot touches the baseline and then the server catches the tossed ball instead of attempting to strike it? This is not a foot fault as long as the server makes no attempt to strike the ball.

USTA Comment 18.5

May a player ask an official how he foot faulted? Yes. The official should then give a brief answer.

USTA Comment 18.6

When may the receiver or the receiver's partner call foot faults? In a non-officiated match, the receiver or the receiver's partner may call foot faults only after all efforts such as warning the server and attempting to locate an official have failed and the foot faulting is so flagrant as to be clearly perceptible from the receiver's side.

---

19. SERVICE FAULT

The service is a fault if:

a. The server breaks Rules 16, 17, or 18; or

b. The server misses the ball when trying to hit it; or

c. The ball served touches a permanent fixture, singles stick or net post before it hits the ground; or

d. The ball served touches the server or server's partner, or anything the server or server's partner is wearing or carrying.

Case 1: After tossing a ball to serve, the server decides not to hit it and catches it instead. Is this a fault?

Decision: No. A player, who tosses the ball and then decides not to hit it, is allowed to catch the ball with the hand or the racket, or to let the ball bounce.

Case 2: During a singles match played on a court with net posts and singles sticks, the ball served hits a singles stick and then hits the correct service court. Is this a fault?

Decision: Yes.

20. SECOND SERVICE

If the first service is a fault, the server shall serve again without delay from behind the same half of the court from which that fault was served, unless the service was from the wrong half.

USTA Comment 20.1
Before returning the second serve, may the receiver clear a ball from a first service fault that has rebounded onto the playing area? Yes.

21. WHEN TO SERVE & RECEIVE

The server shall not serve until the receiver is ready. However, the receiver shall play to the reasonable pace of the server and shall be ready to receive within a reasonable time of the server being ready.

A receiver who attempts to return the service shall be considered as being ready. If it is demonstrated that the receiver is not ready, the service cannot be called a fault.

USTA Comment 21.1
Does this rule apply to the first and second serve? Yes. This rule applies separately to both the first and second serve.

USTA Comment 21.2

Once ready, can the receiver become unready? The receiver cannot become unready unless outside interference occurs.

USTA Comment 21.3

May the server hit the serve just as the receiver looks up after getting into the ready position? No. The receiver is not ready until the receiver is in the ready position and has a second or two to make eye contact with the server.

USTA Comment 21.4

How much time may elapse from the moment the ball goes out of play at the end of the point until the serve is struck to start the next point? When practical this time should not exceed 20 seconds. This limit does not apply if a player has to chase a stray ball.

USTA Comment 21.5

Does the 20-second provision of Rule 29 apply to the second serve? No. The server must strike the second serve without delay.

USTA Comment 21.6

May the server suddenly increase the pace? No. The server may speed up the pace only so long as the new pace is reasonable and only so long as the change does not occur suddenly.

USTA Comment 21.7

What happens when the server observes that the receiver appears to be ready and hits the second serve in, but the receiver makes no attempt to return it? The server wins the point if the receiver had no reason for not being ready; if the receiver was not ready because of something within the receiver's control (broken string or contact lens problem), then the server gets two serves; and if the receiver was not ready because of some reasonable factor such as clearing the errant first serve or a ball from an adjacent court, then the server gets one serve. If the time to clear the ball from the adjacent court is so prolonged as to constitute an interruption, good sportsmanship requires the receiver to offer the server two serves.

22. THE LET DURING A SERVE

The service is a let if:

a. The ball served touches the net, strap or band, and is otherwise good; or, after touching the net, strap or band, touches the receiver or the receiver's partner or anything they wear or carry before hitting the ground; or

b. The ball is served when the receiver is not ready.

In the case of a service let, that particular service shall not count, and the server shall serve again, but a service let does not cancel a previous fault.

Additional approved alternative procedures can be found in Appendix IV.

USTA Comment 22.1
May the receiver claim a let if the server loses control and grip of the racket and it lands during the service in the server's court? No. Such an occurrence is not sufficiently unusual to justify a let.

23. THE LET

In all cases when a let is called, except when a service let is called on a second service, the whole point shall be replayed.

> **Case 1:** When the ball is in play, another ball rolls onto court. A let is called. The server had previously served a fault. Is the server now entitled to a first service or second service?
>
> **Decision:** First service. The whole point must be replayed.

USTA Comment 23.1
What happens when the server is interrupted during delivery of the second service? The server is entitled to two serves.

USTA Comment 23.2
What happens when there is a delay between the first and second serves? If the delay is caused by the receiver (such as a broken string or contact lens problem), an official, or outside interference, the whole point is replayed. If the server caused the delay, such as when the server breaks a string, the server gets one serve. Note that a spectator's call ("out," "fault," or other), a spectator's ringing cell phone, or grunting on an adjacent court is not basis for replaying the point. Action should be taken to prevent further spectator interference.

USTA Comment 23.3
What happens when a ball from an adjacent court rolls on the court between the first and second serves? The time it

takes to clear an intruding ball between the first and second serves is not considered sufficient time to warrant the server receiving two serves unless this time is so prolonged as to constitute an interruption. The receiver is the judge of whether the delay is sufficiently prolonged to justify giving the server two serves.

USTA Comment 23.4
Who may call a let? Only an official or player may call a let. A player may call a let only on the player's court.

24. PLAYER LOSES POINT

The point is lost if:

a.   The player serves two consecutive faults; or

b.   The player does not return the ball in play before it bounces twice consecutively; or

c.   The player returns the ball in play so that it hits the ground, or before it bounces, an object, outside the correct court; or

d.   The player returns the ball in play so that, before it bounces, it hits a permanent fixture; or

e.   The receiver returns the service before it bounces; or

f.   The player deliberately carries or catches the ball in play on the racket or deliberately touches it with the racket more than once; or

g. The player or the racket, whether in the player's hand or not, or anything which the player is wearing or carrying touches the net, net posts/singles sticks, cord or metal cable, strap or band, or the opponent's court at any time while the ball is in play; or

h. The player hits the ball before it has passed the net; or

i. The ball in play touches the player or anything that the player is wearing or carrying, except the racket; or

j. The ball in play touches the racket when the player is not holding it; or

k. The player deliberately and materially changes the shape of the racket when the ball is in play; or

l. In doubles, both players touch the ball when returning it.

Case 1: After the server has served a first service, the racket falls out of the server's hand and touches the net before the ball has bounced. Is this a service fault, or does the server lose the point?

Decision: The server loses the point because the racket touches the net while the ball is in play.

Case 2: After the server has served a first service, the racket falls out of the server's hand and touches the net after the ball has bounced outside the correct service court. Is this a service fault, or does the server lose the point?

Decision: This is a service fault because when the racket touched the net the ball was no longer in play.

Case 3. In a doubles match, the receiver's partner touches the net before the ball that has been served touches the ground outside the correct service court. What is the correct decision?

Decision: The receiving team loses the point because the receiver's partner touched the net while the ball was in play.

Case 4: Does a player lose the point if an imaginary line in the extension of the net is crossed before or after hitting the ball?

Decision: The player does not lose the point in either case provided the player does not touch the opponent's court.

Case 5. Is a player allowed to jump over the net into the opponent's court while the ball is in play?

Decision: No. The player loses the point.

Case 6. A player throws the racket at the ball in play. Both the racket and the ball land in the court on the opponent's side of the net and the opponent(s) is unable to reach the ball. Which player wins the point?

Decision: The player who threw the racket at the ball loses the point.

Case 7. A ball that has just been served hits the receiver or in doubles the receiver's partner before it touches the ground. Which player wins the point?

Decision: The server wins the point, unless it is a service let.

Case 8. A player standing outside the court hits the ball or catches it before it bounces and claims the point because the ball was definitely going out of the correct court.

Decision: The player loses the point, unless it is a good return, in which case the point continues.

USTA Comment 24.1

Does a player lose the point if the player's hat hits the net? Yes. A player loses the point when any part of the player's body, equipment, or apparel touches the net.

USTA Comment 24.2

What happens if the ball hits a player's hat that landed on the court earlier in the point? The ball remains in play because the opponent did not ask for a let. When play continued after the hat landed on the court, the hat became a part of the court. Therefore when a ball hits the hat, it is treated in the same manner as if the ball had hit the court.

USTA Comment 24.3

If a player's hat falls off during a point, may the opponent stop play and claim a let? Yes. The opponent's immediate request should be granted. A let should not be granted after the point nor should a request from the player who lost the hat.

USTA Comment 24.4

What happens if a player's damping device comes out and hits the net or the opponent's court? The player loses the point unless the ball went out of play before the device hit the net or court. If the device is not discovered until after the point is over, the point stands as played.

USTA Comment 24.5

Does a player lose a point if the ball hits his racket twice during one swing? No. Only when there is a definite and deliberate "second push" by the player does the shot become illegal. "Deliberately" is the key word in this rule. Two hits occurring during a single continuous swing are not deemed a double hit.

USTA Comment 24.6

Does the clashing of rackets make the return illegal? No. Unless it is clear that more than one racket touched the ball.

USTA Comment 24.7

Does a player who touches a pipe support that runs across the court at the bottom of the net lose the point? Yes. The pipe support is considered a part of the net except when a ball hits it, in which case the pipe support is considered part of the court.

USTA Comment 24.8

What happens if a player stretches to hit a ball, the racket falls to the ground, and the ball then goes into the court for a winner? The player wins the point unless the racket was not in the player's hand at the instant the ball was struck.

---

25. A GOOD RETURN

It is a good return if:

a.   The ball touches the net, net posts/singles sticks, cord or metal cable, strap or band, provided that it passes over any of them and hits the ground within the correct court; except as provided in Rule 2 and 24 (d); or

b.   After the ball in play has hit the ground within the correct court and has spun or been blown back over the net, the player reaches over the net and plays the ball into the correct court, provided that the player does not break Rule 24; or

c.   The ball is returned outside the net posts, either above or below the level of the top of the net, even though it touches the net posts, provided that it hits the ground in the correct court; except as provided in Rules 2 and 24 (d); or

d.   The ball passes under the net cord between the singles stick and the adjacent net post without touching either net, net cord or net post and hits the ground in the correct court; or

---

e. The player's racket passes over the net after hitting the ball on the player's own side of the net and the ball hits the ground in the correct court; or

f. The player hits the ball in play, which hits another ball lying in the correct court.

Case 1: A player returns a ball which then hits a singles stick and hits the ground in the correct court. Is this is a good return?

Decision: Yes. However, if the ball is served and hits the singles stick, it is a service fault.

Case 2: A ball in play hits another ball which is lying in the correct court. What is the correct decision?

Decision: Play continues. However, if it is not clear that the actual ball in play has been returned, a let should be called.

USTA Comment 25.1
What happens if the ball in play strikes a ball that came from another court after the start of the point? Replay the point.

USTA Comment 25.2
Must a request to remove a ball that is lying in the opponent's court be honored? Yes, but not while the ball is in play. Additionally, a request to remove a ball that is outside the court but reasonably close to the lines also must be honored.

USTA Comment 25.3

In doubles is it a good return if a ball passes under the net cord and inside the post without touching either in a doubles match? No. This is a "through."

USTA Comment 25.4

Does a player lose the point if the opponent's ball touches a pipe support that runs across the court at the bottom of the net? No. The pipe support is considered a part of the court except that it is considered part of the net when a player, or anything the player wears or carries, touches the pipe support.

26. HINDRANCE

If a player is hindered in playing the point by a deliberate act of the opponent(s), the player shall win the point.

However, the point shall be replayed if a player is hindered in playing the point by either an unintentional act of the opponent(s), or something outside the player's own control (not including a permanent fixture).

Case 1: Is an unintentional double hit a hindrance?

Decision: No. See also Rule 24 (f).

Case 2: A player claims to have stopped play because the player thought that the opponent(s) was being hindered. Is this a hindrance?

Decision: No, the player loses the point.

Case 3: A ball in play hits a bird flying over the court. Is this a hindrance?

Decision: Yes, the point shall be replayed.

Case 4: During a point, a ball or other object that was lying on the player's side of the net when the point started hinders the player. Is this a hindrance?

Decision: No.

Case 5: In doubles, where are the server's partner and receiver's partner allowed to stand?

Decision: The server's partner and the receiver's partner may take any position on their own side of the net, inside or outside the court. However, if a player is creating a hindrance to the opponent(s), the hindrance rule should be used.

USTA Comment 26.1
What is the difference between a deliberate and an unintentional act? Deliberate means a player did what the player intended to do, even if the result was unintended. An example is a player who hits a short lob in doubles and loudly shouts "back" just before an opponent hits the overhead. (See The Code § 33.) Unintentional refers to an act over which a player has no control, such as a hat blowing off or a scream after a wasp sting.

USTA Comment 26.2
Can a player's own action be the basis for that player claiming a let or a hindrance? No. Nothing a player does entitles that player to call a let. For example, a player is not entitled to a let because the player breaks a string, the player's hat falls off, or a ball in the player's pocket falls out.

USTA Comment 26.3

What happens if a player's cell phone rings? If the phone rings during the point, the opponent may stop the point and claim the point based on deliberate hindrance. If the cell phone rings between points, the interruption is treated as a Time Violation warning or point penalty depending on whether a previous Time Violation has been issued. In both cases the player shall turn off the cell phone. There is no penalty for a vibrating phone, but the player should immediately turn off the phone unless the Referee has specifically authorized the player to wear a cell phone in vibrate mode.

USTA Comment 26.4

May the Referee authorize a player to wear a cell phone in vibrate mode? Yes. Unless the Referee specifically authorizes a player to wear a cell phone in vibrate mode, any cell phone that is brought to the court must be turned off and placed so that it can be neither seen nor heard. A Referee might authorize a doctor or emergency medical responder who is on call to wear a cell phone in vibrate mode. The Referee should advise the opponent that the player is authorized to wear the cell phone. If the authorized cell phone vibrates during a point, play continues unless the opponent claims a let based on an unintentional hindrance. If a player's cell phone rings, the opponent may stop the point and claim the point on the grounds of a deliberate hindrance.

USTA Comment 26.5

Can the server's discarding of a second ball constitute a hindrance? Yes. If the receiver or an official asks the server to stop discarding the ball, then the server shall stop. Any continued discarding of the ball constitutes a deliberate hindrance, and the server loses the point.

USTA Comment 26.6
Is an out call or other noise from a spectator a hindrance that allows a point to be replayed? No. The actions of a spectator in an area designated for spectators is not the basis for replaying a point.

---

27. CORRECTING ERRORS

As a principle, when an error in respect of the Rules of Tennis is discovered, all points previously played shall stand. Errors so discovered shall be corrected as follows:

a. During a standard game or a tie-break game, if a player serves from the wrong half of the court, this should be corrected as soon as the error is discovered and the server shall serve from the correct half of the court according to the score. A fault that was served before the error was discovered shall stand.

b. During a standard game or a tie-break game, if the players are at the wrong ends of the court, the error should be corrected as soon as it is discovered and the server shall serve from the correct end of the court according to the score.

c. If a player serves out of turn during a standard game, the player who was originally due to serve shall serve as soon as the error is discovered. However, if a game is completed before the error is discovered the order of service shall remain as

---

altered. In this case, any ball change to be made after an agreed number of games should be made one game later than originally scheduled.

A fault that was served by the opponents(s) before the error was discovered shall not stand.

In doubles, if the partners of one team serve out of turn, a fault that was served before the error was discovered shall stand.

d. If a player serves out of turn during a tie-break game and the error is discovered after an even number of points have been played, the error is corrected immediately. If the error is discovered after an odd number of points have been played, the order of service shall remain as altered.

A fault that was served by the opponent(s) before the error was discovered shall not stand.

In doubles, if the partners of one team serve out of turn, a fault that was served before the error was discovered shall stand.

e. During a standard game or a tie-break game in doubles, if there is an error in the order of receiving, this shall remain as altered until the end of the game in which the error is discovered. For the next game in which they are the receivers in that set, the partners shall then resume the original order of receiving.

f. If in error a tie-break game is started at 6 games all, when it was previously agreed that the set would be an "advantage set", the error shall be corrected immediately if only one point has been played. If the error is discovered after the second point is in play, the set will continue as a "tie-break set".

g. If in error a standard game is started at 6 games all, when it was previously agreed that the set would be a "tie-break set", the error shall be corrected immediately if only one point has been played. If the error is discovered after the second point is in play, the set will continue as an "advantage set" until the score reaches 8 games all (or a higher even number), when a tie-break game shall be played.

h. If in error an "advantage set" or "tie-break set" is started, when it was previously agreed that the final set would be a match tie-break, the error shall be corrected immediately if only one point has been played. If the error is discovered after the second point is in play, the set will continue either until a player or team wins three games (and therefore the set) or until the score reaches 2 games all, when a match tie-break shall be played. However, if the error is discovered after the second point of the fifth game has started, the set will continue as a "tie-break set". (See Appendix IV.)

i. If the balls are not changed in the correct sequence, the error shall be corrected when the

player/team who should have served with new
balls is next due to serve a new game. Thereafter
the balls shall be changed so that the number of
games between ball changes shall be that originally agreed. Balls should not be changed during
a game.

USTA Comments on Correcting Errors

USTA Comment 27.1

Errors as to Ends, Sides, Rotation, and Service Order, Etc.
The general guiding philosophy regarding any mistakes
made by players in failing to change ends, serving from
wrong ends, serving to the wrong court, receiving from the
wrong court, etc., is this: Any such error shall be rectified
as soon as discovered but not while the ball is in play, and
any points completed under the erroneous condition shall
be counted.

There are only three exceptions to the "rectify immediately" requirement. One is in the case of a doubles match
where the players of one team happened to reverse their left
court/right court receiving lineup in the middle of a set,
and the switch is discovered in the middle of a game. In
this case the players finish that game in the "new" positions, but resume their original lineup in all receiving
games thereafter in that set.

The second is where a ball change has not taken place
in proper sequence. Rule 27i now says that this mistake
shall be corrected when the player, or pair in case of
doubles, who should have served with the new balls is next
due to serve. Do not change in mid-game.

The third occurs in a tiebreak, either singles or doubles,
in various situations.

USTA Comment 27.2

The tournament announced on its entry form that a 10-Point Match Tiebreak would be used in lieu of the third set. The players inadvertently play a regular set until they realize the mistake at 3-0. What should happen? Since the mistake was discovered before the start of the fifth game, pursuant to Rule 27h the player who is ahead 3-0 has won the set and the final set score should be shown as 3-0.

USTA Comment 27.3

The tournament announced on its entry form that a 10-Point Match Tiebreak would be used in lieu of the third set. The players inadvertently play a regular set until they realize the mistake at 2-1 and 30-all. What should happen? Since the mistake was discovered before the start of the fifth game, the players must continue playing until the score reaches 3-1 or 2-2. If the score reaches 3-1, the player who is ahead wins the set and the final set score is recorded as 3-1. If the score reaches 2-2, a 10-Point Match Tiebreak is played. The score is recorded as 3-2(x) with the score in the 10-Point Match Tiebreak placed inside the parentheses.

USTA Comment 27.4

The tournament announced on its entry form that a 10-Point Match Tiebreak would be used in lieu of the third set. The players inadvertently play a regular set until they realize the mistake after the server has served a first service fault at the beginning of the second point of the fifth game of the final set. What should happen? Regardless of whether the score is 2-2, 3-1, or 4-0, the players must continue playing a full set because they have started the second point of the fifth game. If the score reaches 6-all the players would play a 7-Point Set Tiebreak. The score is recorded the same as any other tiebreak set.

USTA Comment 27.5

Player A should have served the first point of the second set tiebreak, but instead Player B served the first point. Pursuant to Rule 27d, the order of service remained as altered. Who serves the first game of the final set? Player B serves the first game. Rule 5b states that the player whose turn it was to serve first in the set tiebreak shall be the receiver in the first game of the following set.

USTA Comment 27.6

Same situation as in USTA Comment 27.5 except that a 10-Point Match Tiebreak is to be played in lieu of the third set. Who serves first in the 10-Point Match Tiebreak that is to be played in lieu of the final set? Player B.

USTA Comment 27.7

The tournament announced that a 10-Point Match Tiebreak would be played in lieu of the third set. The players split sets. With Player A ahead 7-5, Player A comes to the net to shake hands with Player B. Player B refuses to shake hands because Player B contends that the match tiebreak is not over. What should happen? The players should keep on playing because the 10-Point Match Tiebreak is not yet over.

USTA Comment 27.8

Same situation as in USTA Comment 27.7 except that Player B shakes hands. The players report to the Referee that Player A won the match tiebreak 7-5. Does Player A win the match? Yes. By shaking hands the players have acknowledged that they agreed the match was over. Even though the USTA mandates the use of the 10-Point Match Tiebreak, the 7-Point Tiebreak was played in good faith, so Player A wins the match, and the final set score should be recorded 1-0(5). (See The Code § 2.)

USTA Comment 27.9

Matches in a tournament are supposed to be the best of three tiebreak sets. The players mistakenly start playing a 10-Point Match Tiebreak in lieu of the final set. The error is discovered after Player A has served a first service fault at the beginning of the second point of the 10-Point Match Tiebreak. Should the players continue playing a match tiebreak? Yes. Since the players have started the second point, they must finish the 10-Point Match Tiebreak.

USTA Comment 27.10

What happens if a match is supposed to be played with No-Ad scoring but the players mistakenly use conventional scoring? All games played count. All points count. If the score is deuce when the mistake is discovered, immediately convert to No-Ad scoring. Otherwise continue using conventional scoring until a player wins the game or the score reaches deuce. If the score reaches deuce, the winner of the next point wins the game. (The receiver has the choice of sides except in mixed doubles.)

USTA Comment 27.11

What happens if a match is supposed to be played with short sets but the players mistakenly play a conventional tiebreak set? (First note that a mistake has not occurred unless one player has won five games or unless the score is four-all and the players have started to play the second point of the ninth game.) What should happen depends on the score.

- If the error is discovered when one player leads by two games or more, stop play and the player in the lead wins the set.
- If the error is discovered when one player leads by one game, play one more game or complete the game in progress. If the player now leads by two games, then that player wins the set. If, on the other hand, the set is

now tied, play a 7-Point Set Tiebreak to determine the winner of the set.

- If the error is discovered when the game score is tied and at least one point has been played in the next game, complete the game in progress and one additional game. If one player wins both games, then that player wins the set. If, on the other hand, the score is now tied, play a 7-Point Set Tiebreak to determine the winner of the set.
- If the error is discovered when the score is tied, play a 7-Point Set Tiebreak to determine the winner of the set.

USTA Comment 27.12
The tournament announced on its entry form that the Coman Tiebreak Procedure would be used. The players inadvertently use the conventional procedure. The mistake is discovered at 1-all in the tiebreak. What should happen? Because the mistake was discovered after the players had started playing the second point of the tiebreak, the players finish the set using the conventional tiebreak procedure.

28. ROLE OF COURT OFFICIALS

For matches where officials are appointed, their roles and responsibilities can be found in Appendix V.

29. CONTINUOUS PLAY

As a principle, play should be continuous, from the time the match starts (when the first service of the match is put in play) until the match finishes.

a. Between points, a maximum of twenty (20) seconds is allowed. When the players change ends at the end of a game, a maximum of ninety (90) seconds are allowed. However, after the first game of each set and during a tie-break game, play shall be continuous and the players shall change ends without a rest.

USTA Comment 29.1
The 20-second time limit does not apply if a player has to chase a stray ball. See Rule 21 and USTA Comments 21.1-7 for more information about when the server and receiver must be ready.

At the end of each set there shall be a set break of a maximum of one hundred and twenty (120) seconds.

The maximum time starts from the moment that one point finishes until the first service is struck for the next point.

Event organisers may apply for ITF approval to extend the ninety (90) seconds allowed when the players change ends at the end of a game and the one hundred and twenty (120) seconds allowed at a set break.

b.   If, for reasons outside the player's control, clothing, footwear or necessary equipment (excluding the racket) is broken or needs to be replaced, the player may be allowed reasonable extra time to rectify the problem.

USTA Comment 29.2
Reasonable extra time is determined by the official based on a number of variables such as fairness to the opponent and the distance between the court and a source for replacement clothing, footwear, or equipment. Rarely would more than 15 minutes ever be considered reasonable.

---

c. No extra time shall be given to allow a player to recover condition. However, a player suffering from a treatable medical condition may be allowed one medical timeout of three minutes for the treatment of that medical condition. A limited number of toilet/change of attire breaks may also be allowed, if this is announced in advance of the event.

USTA Comment 29.3
Change of attire breaks are limited to set breaks unless there is a clothing malfunction. Toilet breaks are allowed when an official determines that the need is genuine. They should be taken at set breaks unless there is a true emergency, in which case the break preferably is taken during an odd game changeover, but may be taken immediately. (See Table 11 and USTA Regulation III.F.) Breaks taken at other times should be limited to true emergencies. Gastrointestinal problems are medical conditions that are governed by medical timeout provisions and not by the toilet break provision.

---

d. Event organisers may allow a rest period of a maximum of ten (10) minutes if this is announced in advance of the event. This rest period can be taken after the 3rd set in a best of 5 sets match, or after the 2nd set in a best of 3 sets match.

USTA Comment 29.4
Table 10 in USTA Regulation III.C. sets forth provisions for rest between sets in different divisions.

---

e. The warm-up time shall be a maximum of five (5) minutes, unless otherwise decided by the event organisers.

USTA Comment 29.5
If there are no ball persons, may the warm-up be extended beyond five minutes? Yes. The warm-up may be extended to ten minutes.

USTA Comment 29.6
May play be suspended to replace a lost contact lens? Yes. Whenever possible the player should replace the lens on the court. If the weather, court surface, or other conditions make it impossible to insert the lens on the court, the player should insert the lens in the area closest to the court where this task is possible.

USTA Comment 29.7
When the weather is misty, may play be suspended to allow a player who wears glasses to insert contact lenses? No. The player may change into contacts only on the court and only during a changeover. This case is different from a lost contact lens because the player chose to begin playing the match with glasses.

USTA Comment 29.8
See USTA Comment 4.2 for what happens when a player asks to leave the court to get a replacement racket.

USTA Comment 29.9
When are the players entitled to another warm-up after their match has been suspended? The players are entitled to a re-warm-up of the same duration as the original warm-up

if a match has been suspended for more than 15 minutes. They are not entitled to a re-warm-up after an authorized intermission. When possible, used balls other than the match balls should be used for the re-warm-up, and the match balls should be used only once play resumes. If match balls are used for the re-warm-up and balls are being changed after a designated number of games, the next ball change occurs two games sooner.

USTA Comment 29.10
A best-of-five sets match with an authorized rest period after the third set is suspended because of darkness at one set all. The match is resumed the next day. When Player A wins a long set, Player B claims entitlement to a rest period. Is Player B entitled to a rest period? No. Although this was the third set of the match, it was only the first set on that day. If there is a prolonged interruption, such as one caused by rain, and play is resumed on the same day, the players should be informed as to the point at which, if any, a rest period might later be taken.

---

30. COACHING

Coaching is considered to be communication, advice or instruction of any kind, audible or visible, to a player.

In team events where there is a team captain sitting on-court, the team captain may coach the player(s) during a set break and when the players change ends at the end of a game, but not when the players change ends after the first game of each set and not during a tie-break game.

In all other matches, coaching is not allowed.

Case 1: Is a player allowed to be coached, if the coaching is given by signals in a discreet way?

Decision: No.

Case 2: Is a player allowed to receive coaching when play is suspended?

Decision: Yes.

USTA Comment 30.1

A player may bring to the court written notes that were prepared before the start of the match and may read these notes during the match. A player may not use electronic devices such as cell phones, digital messaging systems, radios, mp3 players, cd and dvd players, cassette players, and any device capable of receiving communication. Hearing aids and watches not capable of receiving messages are permitted. A player desiring to use any other electronic device should first ask the Referee whether the device may be used.

USTA Comment 30.2

Is coaching permitted during authorized rest periods? Yes. However, an authorized rest period does not include a toilet break, a 2-minute set break, medical timeout, bleeding timeout, when play is suspended but the players remain on the court, when a player leaves the court seeking the assistance of the Referee, or when equipment or clothing is being adjusted.

USTA Comment 30.3

Is coaching permitted in the USTA League programs? No. Even though the USTA League programs are team competitions for adults and seniors, coaching is not permitted under league rules, except during authorized rest periods or as otherwise permitted.

Rules of
Wheelchair
Tennis

The game of wheelchair tennis follows the ITF Rules of Tennis with the following exceptions.

a. **The Two Bounce Rule**

The wheelchair tennis player is allowed two bounces of the ball. The player must return the ball before it bounces a third time. The second bounce can be either in or out of the court boundaries.

b. **The Wheelchair**

The wheelchair is considered part of the body and all applicable rules, which apply to a player's body, shall apply to the wheelchair.

c. **The Service**

The service shall be delivered in the following manner:

i. Immediately before commencing the service, the server shall be in a stationary position. The server shall then be allowed one push before striking the ball.

ii. The server shall throughout the delivery of the service not touch with any wheel, any area other than that behind the baseline within the imaginary extension of the centre mark and sideline.

iii. If conventional methods for the service are physically impossible for a quad player, then the player or another individual may drop the ball for such a player and allow it to bounce before it is struck. If this is the case, the same method of serving must be used for the entire match.

d. **Player Loses Point**

A player loses a point if:

i. The player fails to return the ball before it has bounced three times; or

ii. Subject to rule e) below the player uses any part of his feet or lower extremities against the ground or against any wheel while delivering service, stroking a ball, turning or stopping against the ground or against any wheel while the ball is in play; or

iii. The player fails to keep one buttock in contact with his wheelchair seat when contacting the ball.

e. **Propelling the Chair with the Foot**

i. If due to lack of capacity a player is unable to propel the wheelchair via the wheel then he may propel the wheelchair using one foot.

ii. Even if in accordance with rule e) i. above a player is permitted to propel the chair using one foot, no part of the player's foot may be in contact with the ground:

a) during the forward motion of the swing, including when the racket strikes the ball;

b) from the initiation of the service motion until the racket strikes the ball.

iii. A player in breach of this rule shall lose the point.

f. **Wheelchair/Able-bodied Tennis**

Where a wheelchair tennis player is playing with or against an able-bodied person in singles or doubles, the Rules of Wheelchair Tennis shall apply for the wheelchair player while the Rules of Tennis for able-bodied tennis shall apply for the able-bodied player. In this instance, the wheelchair player is allowed two bounces while the able-bodied player is allowed only one bounce.

Note: The definition of lower extremities is: the lower limbs, including the buttocks, hips, thighs, legs, ankles and feet.

Amendment to the Rules of Tennis

The official and decisive text to the Rules of Tennis shall be for ever in the English language and no alteration or interpretation of such Rules shall be made except at an Annual General Meeting of the Council, nor unless notice of the resolution embodying such alteration shall have been received by the Federation in accordance with Article 17 of the Constitution of ITF Ltd (Notice of Resolutions) and such resolution or one having the like effect shall be carried by a majority of two-thirds of the votes recorded in respect of the same.

Any alteration so made shall take effect as from the first day of January following unless the Meeting shall by the like majority decide otherwise.

The Board of Directors shall have power, however, to settle all urgent questions of interpretation subject to confirmation at the General Meeting next following.

This Rule shall not be altered at any time without the unanimous consent of a General Meeting of the Council.

USTA Comment

The ITF, not the USTA, is responsible for the Rules of Tennis. Amendments to the Rules of Tennis are made through the procedures of the ITF. Rule 69 of the ITF controls the manner in which amendments may be made to the Rules of Tennis. Amendments to USTA Comments are made by the process described in USTA Regulation XIX.H.

Appendixes

APPENDIX I
THE BALL

For all measurements in Appendix I, SI units shall take precedence.

a. The ball shall have a uniform outer surface consisting of a fabric cover and shall be white or yellow in colour. If there are any seams they shall be stitchless.

b. More than one type of ball is specified. The ball shall conform to the requirements shown in Table 1.

Table 1. Tennis Ball Specification

	TYPE 1 (FAST)	TYPE 2 (MEDIUM)[1]	TYPE 3 (SLOW)[2]	HIGH ALTITUDE[3]
Weight (Mass)	1.975-2.095 oz. (56.0-59.4 g.)	1.975-2.095 oz. (56.0-59.4 g.)	1.975-2.095 oz. (56.0-59.4 g.)	1.975-2.095 oz. (56.0-59.4 g.)
Size	2.575-2.700 in. (6.541-6.858 cm)	2.575-2.700 in. (6.541-6.858 cm)	2.750-2.875 in. (6.985-7.303 cm)	2.575-2.700 in. (6.541-6.858 cm)
Rebound	53-58 in. (135-147 cm)	53-58 in. (135-147 cm)	53-58 in. (135-147 cm)	48-53 in. (122-135 cm)
Forward Deformation[4]	0.195-0.235 in. (0.495-0.597 cm)	0.220-0.290 in. (0.559-0.737 cm)	0.220-0.290 in. (0.559-0.737 cm)	0.220-0.290 in. (0.559-0.737 cm)
Return Deformation[4]	0.265-0.360 in. (0.673-0.914 cm)	0.315-0.425 in. (0.800-1.080 cm)	0.315-0.425 in. (0.800-1.080 cm)	0.315-0.425 in. (0.800-1.080 cm)

Notes:

1. This ball may be pressurised or pressureless. The pressureless ball shall have an internal pressure that is no greater than 1 psi (7 kPa) and may be used for high altitude play above 4,000 feet (1,219 m) above sea level and shall have been acclimatised for 60 days or more at the altitude of the specific tournament.

2. This ball is also recommended for high altitude play on any court surface type above 4,000 feet (1,219 m) above sea level.

3. This ball is pressurised and is an additional ball specified for high altitude play above 4,000 feet (1,219 m) above sea level only.

4. The deformation shall be the average of a single reading along each of three perpendicular axes. No two individual readings shall differ by more than .030 inches (.076 cm).

c. All tests for rebound, size and deformation shall be made in accordance with the Regulations for making tests.

	Weight (Mass)	Rebound	Foreward Deformation	Return Deformation
Maximum	0.014 oz.	1.6 inches	0.031 inches	0.039 inches
Change[1]	(0.4 g.)	(4.0 cm.)	(0.08 cm.)	(0.10 cm.)

Notes:

1 The largest permissible change in the specified properties resulting from the durability test described in the current edition of ITF Approved Tennis Balls & Classified Court Surfaces. The durability test uses laboratory equipment to simulate the effects of nine games of play.

d. All tests for rebound, mass, size, deformation and durability shall be made in accordance with the Regulations described in the current edition of ITF Approved Tennis Balls & Classified Court Surfaces.

CLASSIFICATION OF COURT PACE

The ITF test method used for determining the pace of a court surface is ITF CS 01/02 (ITF Court Pace Rating) as described in the ITF publication entitled "ITF guide to test methods for tennis court surfaces".

Court surfaces which have an ITF Court Pace Rating of 0 to 29 shall be classified as being Category 1 (slow pace). Examples of court surface types which conform to this classification will include most clay courts and other types of unbound mineral surface.

Court surfaces which have an ITF Court Pace Rating of 30 to 34 shall be classified as being Category 2 (medium-slow pace), while court surfaces with an ITF Court Pace Rating of 35 to 39 shall be classified as being Category 3 (medium pace). Examples of court surface types which conform to this classification will include most acrylic coated surfaces plus some carpet surfaces.

Court surfaces with an ITF Court Pace Rating of 40 to 44 shall be classified as being Category 4 (medium-fast pace), while court surfaces which have an ITF Court Pace Rating of 45 or more shall be classified as being Category 5 (fast pace). Examples of court surface types which conform to this classification will include most natural grass, artificial grass and some carpet surfaces.

Case 1: Which ball type should be used on which court surface?

Decision: 3 different types of balls are approved for play under the Rules of Tennis, however:

a. Ball Type 1 (fast speed) is intended for play on slow pace court surfaces.

b. Ball Type 2 (medium speed) is intended for play on medium-slow, medium, and medium-fast pace court surfaces.

c. Ball Type 3 (slow speed) is intended for play on fast pace court surfaces.

APPENDIX II
THE RACKET

For all measurements in Appendix II, SI units shall take precedence.

a. The hitting surface, defined as the main area of the stringing pattern bordered by the points of entry of the strings into the frame or points of contact of the strings with the frame, whichever is the smaller, shall be flat and consist of a pattern of crossed strings connected to a frame and alternately interlaced or bonded where they cross. The stringing pattern must be generally uniform and, in particular, not less dense in the centre than in any other area.

    The racket shall be designed and strung such that the playing characteristics are identical on both faces. The racket shall be free of attached objects, protrusions and devices other than those utilised solely and specifically to limit or prevent wear and tear or vibration or, for the frame only, to distribute weight. These objects, protrusions and devices must be reasonable in size and placement for such purposes.

b. The frame of the racket shall not exceed 73.7 cm (29.0 inches) in overall length, including the handle. The frame of the racket shall not exceed 31.7 cm (12.5 inches) in overall width. The hitting surface shall not exceed 39.4 cm (15.5 inches) in overall length, and 29.2 cm (11.5 inches) in overall width.

c. The frame, including the handle, and the strings, shall be free of any device which makes it possible to change materially the shape of the racket, or to change materially the weight distribution in the direction of the longitudinal axis of the racket which would alter the swing moment of inertia, or to change deliberately any physical property which may affect the performance of the racket during the playing of a point. No energy source that in any way changes or affects the playing characteristics of a racket may be built into or attached to a racket.

d. The racket must be free of any device that may provide communication, advice or instruction of any kind, audible or visible, to a player during a match.

APPENDIX III
ADVERTISING

1. Advertising is permitted on the net as long as it is placed on the part of the net that is within 3 feet (0.914 m) from the centre of the net posts and is produced in such a way that it does not interfere with the vision of the players or the playing conditions.

2. Advertising and other marks or material placed at the back and sides of the court shall be permitted unless it interferes with the vision of the players or the playing conditions.

3. Advertising and other marks or material placed on the court surface outside the lines is permitted unless it interferes with the vision of the players or the playing conditions.

4. Notwithstanding paragraphs (1), (2) and (3) above, any advertising, marks or material placed on the net or placed at the back and sides of the court, or on the court surface outside the lines may not contain white or yellow or other light colours that may interfere with the vision of the players or the playing conditions.

5. Advertising and other marks or material are not permitted on the court surface inside the lines of the court.

APPENDIX IV
ALTERNATIVE SCORING PROCEDURES
AND METHODS

SCORE IN A GAME (RULE 5):
"No-Ad" SCORING METHOD

This alternative scoring method may be used.

A No-Ad game is scored as follows with the server's score being called first:

No point	"Love"
First point	"15"
Second point	"30"
Third point	"40"
Fourth point	"Game"

If both players/teams have won three points each, the score is "deuce" and a deciding point shall be played. The receiver(s) shall choose whether to receive the service from the right half or the left half of the court. In doubles, the players of the receiving team cannot change positions to receive this deciding point. The player/team who wins the deciding point wins the "game".

In mixed doubles, the player of the same gender as the server shall receive the deciding point. The players of the receiving team cannot change positions to receive the deciding point.

USTA Comment IV.1

USTA Regulation III.G.1. authorizes the Referee to switch to No-Ad scoring before the start of any round without prior notice in all tournaments other than USTA Junior National Championships and USTA Regional Tournaments after inclement weather or other factors cause the tournament to fall behind its published schedule.

USTA Comment IV.2

Traditional scoring or numeric scoring may be used with the No-Ad scoring method.

SCORE IN A SET (RULES 6 AND 7):

1. **"Short" Sets**

   The first player/team who wins four games wins that set, provided there is a margin of two games over the opponent(s). If the score reaches four games all, a tie-break game shall be played.

2. **Match Tie-Break (7 Points)**

   When the score in a match is one set all, or two sets all in best of five sets matches, one tie-break game shall be played to decide the match. This tie-break game replaces the deciding final set.

   The player/team who first wins seven points shall win this match tie-break and the match provided there is a margin of two points over the opponent(s).

USTA Comment IV.3
USTA Regulation I.E.1.b. prohibits the playing of a 7-Point Tiebreak as the match tiebreak.

3. **Match Tie-break (10 Points)**

    When the score in a match is one set all, or two sets all in best of five sets matches, one tie-break game shall be played to decide the match. This tie-break game replaces the deciding final set.

    The player/team who first wins ten points shall win this match tie-break and the match provided there is a margin of two points over the opponent(s).

Note: When using the match tie-break to replace the final set:

- the original order of service continues. (Rules 5 and 14)

- in doubles, the order of serving and receiving within the team may be altered, as in the beginning of each set. (Rules 14 and 15)

- before the start of the match tie-break there shall be a 120 seconds set break.

- balls should not be changed before the start of the match tie-break even if a ball change is due.

CHANGE OF ENDS (RULE 10)
(COMAN TIE-BREAK):

This alternative to the change of ends sequence in a tie-break game may be used.

During a tie-break game, players shall change ends after the first point and thereafter after every four points.

THE LET DURING A SERVICE (RULE 22):

This alternative is play without the service let in Rule 22a.

It means that a serve that touches the net, strap or band, is in play.

(This alternative is commonly known as the "no let rule.")

USTA Comment IV.4
If the previous set did not go to a tiebreak, under Rule 14 the order of service continues. If the previous set went to a tiebreak, under Rule 5 the player or team that was scheduled to serve first in the tiebreak receives first in the 10-Point Match Tiebreak.

USTA Comment IV.5
USTA Regulation I.E.1.b. authorizes the 10-Point Match Tiebreak in lieu of a deciding final set. USTA Regulation III.G.2. explains when the Referee may switch the match format to a 10-Point Match Tiebreak in lieu of a deciding final set.

Table 17 lists the tournaments on the National Junior Tournament Schedule in which the 10-Point Match Tiebreak is played in lieu of a deciding final set. If there is inclement weather, health concerns, or safety concerns, the Director of Junior Competition or the Director's Designee may authorize the Referee to play a 10-Point Match Tiebreak in lieu of a deciding final set at USTA Junior National Championships and USTA Regional Tournaments. (See USTA Regulation IX.A.7.)

USTA Regulation X.A.2.d. and h. explains when 10-Point Match Tiebreaks may be played in lieu of a deciding final set at Category I USTA Adult, Senior, and Family National Championships. USTA Regulation XIII.A.3.d. and h. explains when 10-Point Match Tiebreaks may be played in lieu of a deciding final set at Category I USTA Wheelchair National Championships.

APPENDIX V
ROLE OF COURT OFFICIALS

The Referee is the final authority on all questions of tennis law and the Referee's decision is final.

In matches where a Chair Umpire is assigned, the Chair Umpire is the final authority on all questions of fact during the match.

The players have the right to call the Referee to court if they disagree with a Chair Umpire's interpretation of tennis law.

In matches where Line Umpires and Net Umpires are assigned, they make all calls (including foot-fault calls) relating to that line or net. The Chair Umpire has the right to overrule a Line Umpire or a Net Umpire if the Chair Umpire is sure that a clear mistake has been made. The Chair Umpire is responsible for calling any line (including foot-faults) or net where no Line Umpire or Net Umpire is assigned.

A Line Umpire who cannot make a call shall signal this immediately to the Chair Umpire who shall make a decision. If the Line Umpire can not make a call, or if there is no Line Umpire, and the Chair Umpire can not make a decision on a question of fact, the point shall be replayed.

In team events where the Referee is sitting on-court, the Referee is also the final authority on questions of fact.

Play may be stopped or suspended at any time the Chair Umpire decides it is necessary or appropriate.

The Referee may also stop or suspend play in the case of darkness, weather or adverse court conditions. When play is suspended for darkness, this should be done at the end of a set, or after an even number of games have been played in the set in progress. After a suspension in play, the score and position of players on-court in the match shall stand when the match resumes.

The Chair Umpire or Referee shall make decisions regarding continuous play and coaching in respect of any Code of Conduct that is approved and in operation.

Case 1: The Chair Umpire awards the server a first service after an overrule, but the receiver argues that it should be a second service, since the server had already served a fault. Should the Referee be called to court to give a decision?

Decision: Yes. The Chair Umpire makes the first decision about questions of tennis law (issues relating to the application of specific facts). However, if a player appeals the Chair Umpire's decision, then the Referee shall be called to make the final decision.

Case 2: A ball is called out, but a player claims that the ball was good. May the Referee be called to court to make a decision?

Decision: No. The Chair Umpire makes the final decision on questions of fact (issues relating to what actually happened during a specific incident).

Case 3: Is a Chair Umpire allowed to overrule a Line Umpire at the end of a point if, in the Chair Umpire's opinion, a clear mistake was made earlier in the point?

Decision: No. A Chair Umpire may only overrule a Line Umpire immediately after the clear mistake has been made.

Case 4: A Line Umpire calls a ball "Out" and then the player argues that the ball was good. Is the Chair Umpire allowed to overrule the Line Umpire?

Decision: No. A Chair Umpire must never overrule as the result of the protest or appeal by a player.

Case 5: A Line Umpire calls a ball "Out". The Chair Umpire was unable to see clearly, but thought the ball was in. May the Chair Umpire overrule the Line Umpire?

Decision: No. The Chair Umpire may only overrule when sure that the Line Umpire made a clear mistake.

Case 6: Is a Line Umpire allowed to change the call after the Chair Umpire has announced the score?

Decision: Yes. If a Line Umpire realises a mistake, a correction should be made as soon as possible provided it is not as the result of a protest or appeal of a player.

Case 7: If a Chair Umpire or Line Umpire calls "out" and then corrects the call to good, what is the correct decision?

Decision: The Chair Umpire must decide if the original "out" call was a hindrance to either player. If it was a hindrance, the point shall be replayed. If it was not a hindrance, the player who hit the ball wins the point.

Case 8: A ball is blown back over the net and the player correctly reaches over the net to try to play the ball. The opponent(s) hinders the player from doing this. What is the correct decision?

Decision: The Chair Umpire must decide if the hindrance was deliberate or unintentional and either awards the point to the hindered player or order the point to be replayed.

USTA Comment V.1
What is the difference between a "question of fact" and a "question of law"? "Questions of fact" involve whether a specific event happened. Examples include whether a ball is in, whether a ball touched a player, whether a ball bounced twice, and whether a server's foot touched the baseline before the serve was struck. "Questions of law" involve the application of the rules or regulations to facts that have already been determined. Examples include determining whether an act was a hindrance; whether a player should have been assessed a code violation for misconduct; and the procedure for correcting errors in serving order, serving and receiving position, and ends.

BALL MARK INSPECTION PROCEDURES

1. Ball mark inspections can only be made on clay courts.

---

2. A ball mark inspection requested by a player (team) shall be allowed only if the Chair Umpire cannot determine the call with certainty from his/her chair on either a point-ending shot or when a player (team) stops playing the point during a rally (returns are permitted but then the player must immediately stop).

3. When the Chair Umpire has decided to make a ball mark inspection, he/she should go down from the chair and make the inspection himself. If he/she does not know where the mark is, he/she can ask the Line Umpire for help in locating the mark, but then the Chair Umpire shall inspect it.

4. The original call or overrule will always stand if the Line Umpire and Chair Umpire cannot determine the location of the mark or if the mark is unreadable.

5. Once the Chair Umpire has identified and ruled on a ball mark, this decision is final and not appealable.

6. In clay court tennis the Chair Umpire should not be too quick to announce the score unless absolutely certain of the call. If in doubt, wait before calling the score to determine whether a ball mark inspection is necessary.

7. In doubles the appealing player must make his/her appeal in such a way that either play

stops or the Chair Umpire stops play. If an appeal is made to the Chair Umpire then he/she must first determine that the correct appeal procedure was followed. If it was not correct or if it was late, then the Chair Umpire may determine that the opposing team was deliberately hindered.

8. If a player erases the ball mark before the Chair Umpire has made a final decision, he/she concedes the call.

9. A player may not cross the net to check a ball mark without being subject to the Unsportsmanlike provision of the Code of Conduct.

USTA Comment V.2.
See FAC Comment VII.C-6 for additional procedures.

ELECTRONIC REVIEW PROCEDURES

At tournaments where an Electronic Review System is used, the following procedures should be followed for matches on courts where it is used.

1. A request for an Electronic Review of a line call or overrule by a player (team) shall be allowed only on either a point-ending shot or when a player (team) stops playing the point during a rally (returns are permitted but then the player must immediately stop).

---

2. The Chair Umpire should decide to use the Electronic Review when there is doubt about the accuracy of the line call or overrule. However, the Chair Umpire may refuse the Electronic Review if he/she believes that the player is making an unreasonable request or that it was not made in a timely manner.

3. In doubles the appealing player must make his/her appeal in such a way that either play stops or the Chair Umpire stops play. If an appeal is made to the Chair Umpire then he/she must first determine that the correct appeal procedure was followed. If it was not correct or if it was late, then the Chair Umpire may determine that the opposing team was deliberately hindered, in which case the appealing team loses the point.

4. The original call or overrule will always stand if the Electronic Review is unable, for whatever reason, to make a decision on that line call or overrule.

5. The Chair Umpire's final decision will be the outcome of the Electronic Review and is not appealable. If a manual choice is required for the system to review a particular ball impact, a review official approved by the Referee shall ecide which ball impact is reviewed. 6.

Each player (team) is allowed three (3) unsuccessful appeals per set, plus one (1) additional appeal in the tie-break. For matches with advantage sets, players (teams) will start again with a maximum of 3 unsuccessful appeals at 6 games all and every 12 games thereafter. For matches with match tie-break, the match tie-break counts as a new set and each player (team) starts with three (3) appeals. Players (teams) will have an unlimited number of successful appeals.

APPENDIX VI
10 AND UNDER TENNIS COMPETITION

COURTS

In addition to the (full sized) court described in Rule 1, the following court dimensions may be used for 10 and under tennis competition:

- A court, designated "red" for the purpose of 10 and under tennis competition, shall be a rectangle, between 36 feet (10.97 m) and 42 feet (12.80 m) long, and between 16 feet (4.88 m) and 20 feet (6.10 m) wide. The net shall be between 31.5 inches (0.800 m) and 33.0 inches (0.838 m) high at the centre.

- A court, designated "orange", shall be a rectangle, between 59 feet (17.98 m) and 60 feet (18.29 m) long, and between 21 feet (6.40 m) and 27 feet (8.23 m) wide. The net shall be between 31.5 inches (0.800 m) and 36.0 inches (0.914 m) high at the centre.

BALLS

From January 2012, only the following ball types can be used in 10 and under tennis competition:

- A stage 3 (red) ball, which is recommended for play on a "red" court, by players aged up to 8 years, using a racket up to 23 inches (58.4 cm) long.

- A stage 2 (orange) ball, which is recommended for play on an "orange" court, by players aged 8 to 10 years, using a racket between 23 inches (58.4 cm) and 25 inches (63.5 cm) long.

- A stage 1 (green) ball, which is recommended for play on a full sized court, by advanced players aged 9 to 10 years, using a racket between 25 inches (63.5 cm) and 26 inches (66.0 cm) long.

Note: From January 2012, other ball types described in Appendix I cannot be used in 10 and under tennis competition.

Specifications for Stage 1, 2 and 3 Balls:
All tests for rebound, mass, size and deformation shall be made in accordance with the regulations described in the current edition of ITF Approved Tennis Balls & Classified Court Surfaces.

SCORING METHODS

For 10 and under tennis competition using stage 3 (red), stage 2 (orange) or stage 1 (green) balls, scoring methods specified in the Rules of Tennis (including the Appendix IV) can be utilised, in addition to short duration scoring methods involving matches of one match tie-break, best of 3 tie-breaks/match tie-breaks or one set.

USTA Comment V.1.
See USTA Regulation VI., which contains additional provisions for 10 and under tennis competition.

APPENDIX VII
PROCEDURES FOR REVIEW AND HEARINGS
ON THE RULES OF TENNIS

1. INTRODUCTION

1.1 These procedures were approved by the Board of Directors of the International Tennis Federation ("Board of Directors") on 17 May 1998.

1.2 The Board of Directors may from time to time supplement, amend, or vary these procedures.

2. OBJECTIVES

2.1 The International Tennis Federation is the custodian of the Rules of Tennis and is committed to:

   a. Preserving the traditional character and integrity of the game of tennis.

   b. Actively preserving the skills traditionally required to play the game.

   c. Encouraging improvements, which maintain the challenge of the game.

   d. Ensuring fair competition.

2.2 To ensure fair, consistent and expeditious review and hearings in relation to the Rules of Tennis the procedures set out below shall apply.

3. SCOPE

3.1 These Procedures shall apply to Rulings under:

    a.   Rule 1—The Court.

    b.   Rule 3—The Ball.

    c.   Rule 4—The Racket.

    d.   Appendix I and II of the Rules of Tennis.

    e.   Any other Rules of Tennis which the International Tennis Federation may decide.

4. STRUCTURE

4.1 Under these procedures Rulings shall be issued by a Ruling Board.

4.2 Such Rulings shall be final save, for an entitlement to appeal to an Appeal Tribunal pursuant to these procedures.

5. APPLICATION

5.1 Rulings shall be taken either:

    a.   Following a motion of the Board of Directors; or

    b.   Upon the receipt of an application in accordance with the procedures set out below.

6. APPOINTMENT AND COMPOSITION OF RULING BOARDS

6.1 Ruling Boards shall be appointed by the President of the International Tennis Federation ("President") or his designee and shall comprise of such a number, as the President or his designee shall determine.

6.2 If more than one person is appointed to the Ruling Board the Ruling Board shall nominate one person from amongst themselves to act as Chairperson.

6.3 The Chairperson shall be entitled to regulate the procedures prior to and at any review and/or hearing of a Ruling Board.

7. PROPOSED RULINGS BY THE RULING BOARD

7.1 The details of any proposed Ruling issued upon the motion of the Board of Directors may be provided to any bona fide person or any players, equipment manufacturer or national association or members thereof with an interest in the proposed Ruling.

7.2 Any person so notified shall be given a reasonable period within which to forward comments, objections, or requests for information to the President or his designee in connection with the proposed Ruling.

8. APPLICATION FOR RULINGS

8.1 An application for a Ruling may be made by any party with a bona fide interest in the Ruling including any player, equipment manufacturer or national association or member thereof.

8.2 Any application for a Ruling must be submitted in writing to the President.

8.3 To be valid an application for a Ruling must include the following minimum information:

a. The full name and address of the Applicant.

b. The date of the application.

c. A statement clearly identifying the interest of the Applicant in the question upon which a Ruling is requested.

d. All relevant documentary evidence upon which the Applicant intends to rely at any hearing.

e. If, in the opinion of the Applicant, expert evidence is necessary he shall include a request for such expert evidence to be heard. Such request must identify the name of any expert proposed and their relevant expertise.

f. When an application for a Ruling on a racket or other piece of equipment is made, a prototype or, exact, copy of the equipment in question must be submitted with the application for a Ruling.

g.   If, in the opinion of the Applicant, there are extraordinary or unusual circumstances, which require a Ruling to be made within a specified time or before a specified date he shall include a statement describing the extraordinary or unusual circumstances.

8.4 If an application for a Ruling does not contain the information and/or equipment referred to at Clause 8.3 (a)-(g) above the President or his designee shall notify the Applicant giving the Applicant a specified reasonable time within which to remedy the defect. If the Applicant fails to remedy the defect within the specified time the application shall be dismissed.

9.   CONVENING THE RULING BOARD

9.1 On receipt of a valid application or on the motion of the Board of Directors the President or his designee may convene a Ruling Board to deal with the application or motion.

9.2 The Ruling Board need not hold a hearing to deal with an application or motion where the application or motion, in the opinion of the Chairperson can be resolved in a fair manner without a hearing.

10. PROCEDURE OF THE RULING BOARD

10.1 The Chairperson of a Ruling Board shall determine the appropriate form, procedure and date of any review and/or hearing.

10.2 The Chairperson shall provide written notice of those matters set out at 10.1 above to any Applicant or any person or association who has expressed an interest in the proposed Ruling.

10.3 The Chairperson shall determine all matters relating to evidence and shall not be bound by judicial rules governing procedure and admissibility of evidence provided that the review and/or hearing is conducted in a fair manner with a reasonable opportunity for the relevant parties to present their case.

10.4 Under these procedures any review and/or hearings:

a. Shall take place in private.

b. May be adjourned and/or postponed by the Ruling Board.

10.5 The Chairperson shall have the discretion to co-opt from time to time additional members onto the Ruling Board with special skill or experience to deal with specific issues, which require such special skill or experience.

10.6 The Ruling Board shall take its decision by a simple majority. No member of the Ruling Board may abstain.

10.7 The Chairperson shall have the complete discretion to make such order against the Applicant [and/or other individuals or organisations commenting objecting or requesting information at any review and/or hearing] in relation to the costs of the application and/or the reasonable expenses incurred by the Ruling Board in holding tests or obtaining reports relating to equipment subject to a Ruling as he shall deem appropriate.

11. NOTIFICATION

11.1 Once a Ruling Board has reached a decision it shall provide written notice to the Applicant, or, any person or association who has expressed an interest in the proposed Ruling as soon as reasonably practicable.

11.2 Such written notice shall include a summary of the reasoning behind the decision of the Ruling Board.

11.3 Upon notification to the Applicant or upon such other date specified by the Ruling Board the Ruling of the Ruling Board shall be immediately binding under the Rules of Tennis.

12. APPLICATION OF CURRENT RULES OF TENNIS

12.1 Subject to the power of the Ruling Board to issue interim Rulings the current Rules of Tennis shall continue to apply until any review and/or hearing of the Ruling Board is concluded and a Ruling issued by the Ruling Board.

12.2 Prior to and during any review and/or hearing the Chairperson of the Ruling Board may issue such directions as are deemed reasonably necessary in the implementation of the Rules of Tennis and of these procedures including the issue of interim Rulings.

12.3 Such interim Rulings may include restraining orders on the use of any equipment under the Rules of Tennis pending a Ruling by the Ruling Board as to whether or not the equipment meets the specification of the Rules of Tennis.

13. APPOINTMENT AND COMPOSITION OF APPEAL TRIBUNALS

13.1 Appeal Tribunals shall be appointed by the President or his designee from [members of the Board of Directors/Technical Commission].

13.2 No member of the Ruling Board who made the original Ruling shall be a member of the Appeal Tribunal.

13.3 The Appeal Tribunal shall comprise of such number as the President or his designee shall determine but shall be no less than three.

13.4 The Appeal Tribunal shall nominate one person from amongst themselves to act as Chairperson.

13.5 The Chairperson shall be entitled to regulate the procedures prior to and at any appeal hearing.

14. APPLICATION TO APPEAL

14.1 An Applicant [or a person or association who has expressed an interest and forwarded any comments, objections, or requests to a proposed Ruling] may appeal any Ruling of the Ruling Board.

14.2 To be valid an application for an appeal must be:

a. Made in writing to the Chairperson of the Ruling Board who made the Ruling appealed not later than [45] days following notification of the Ruling;

b. Must set out details of the Ruling appealed against; and

c. Must contain the full grounds of the appeal.

14.3 Upon receipt of a valid application to appeal the Chairperson of the Ruling Board making the original Ruling may require a reasonable appeal fee to be paid by the Appellant as a condition of appeal. Such appeal fee shall be repaid to the Appellant if the appeal is successful.

15. CONVENING THE APPEAL TRIBUNAL

15.1 The President or his designee shall convene the Appeal Tribunal following payment by the Appellant of any appeal fee.

16. PROCEDURES OF APPEAL TRIBUNAL

16.1 The Appeal Tribunal and their Chairperson shall conduct procedures and hearings in accordance with those matters set out in sections 10, 11 and 12 above.

16.2 Upon notification to the Appellant or upon such other date specified by the Appeal Tribunal the Ruling of the Appeal Tribunal shall be immediately binding and final under the Rules of Tennis.

17. GENERAL

17.1 If a Ruling Board consists of only one member that single member shall be responsible for regulating the hearing as Chairperson and shall determine the procedures to be followed prior to and during any review and/or hearing.

17.2 All review and/or hearings shall be conducted in English. In any hearing where an Applicant, and/or other individuals or organisations commenting, objecting or requesting information do not speak English an interpreter must be present. Wherever practicable the interpreter shall be independent.

17.3 The Ruling Board or Appeal Tribunal may publish extracts from its own Rulings.

17.4 All notifications to be made pursuant to these procedures shall be in writing.

17.5 Any notifications made pursuant to these procedures shall be deemed notified upon the date that they were communicated, sent or transmitted to the Applicant or other relevant party.

17.6 A Ruling Board shall have the discretion to dismiss an application if in its reasonable opinion the application is substantially similar to an application or motion upon which a Ruling Board has made a decision and/or Ruling within the 36 months prior to the date of the application.

APPENDIX VIII
PLAN OF THE COURT

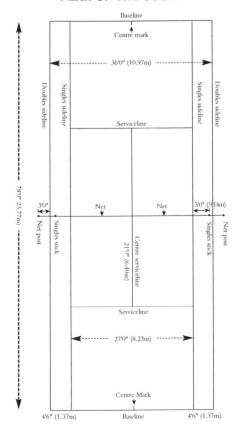

FIG. 1

APPENDIX IX
SUGGESTIONS ON HOW TO MARK OUT A COURT

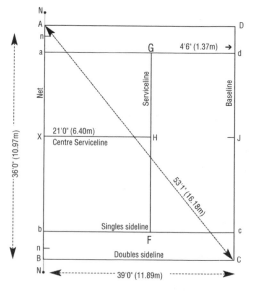

FIG. 2

Note: All court measurements shall be made to the outside of the lines.

The following procedure is for the usual combined doubles and singles court. (See note at foot for a court for one purpose only.)

First select the position of the net; a straight line 42 feet (12.80 m) long. Mark the centre (X on the diagram above) and, measuring from there in each direction, mark:

at 13'6" (4.11 m) the points a, b, where the net crosses the inner sidelines,

at 16'6" (5.03 m) the positions of the singles sticks (n, n),

at 18'0" (5.48 m) the points A, B, where the net crosses the outer sidelines,

at 21'0" (6.40 m) the positions of the net posts (N, N), being the ends of the original 42'0" (12.80 m) line.

Insert pegs at A and B and attach to them the respective ends of two measuring tapes. On one, which will measure the diagonal of the half-court, take a length 53'1" (16.18 m) and on the other (to measure the sideline) a length of 39'0" (11.89 m). Pull both taut so that at these distances they meet at a point C, which is one corner of the court. Reverse the measurements to find the other corner D. As a check on this operation it is advisable at this stage to verify the length of the line CD which, being the baseline, should be found to be 36'0" (10.97m); and at the same time its centre J can be marked, and also the ends of the inner sidelines (c, d), 4'6" (1.37 m) from C and D.

The centreline and serviceline are now marked by means of the points F, H, G, which are measured 21'0" (6.40 m) from the net down the lines bc, XJ, ad, respectively.

Identical procedure the other side of the net completes the court.

If a singles court only is required, no lines are necessary outside the points a, b, c, d, but the court can be measured out as above. Alternatively, the corners of the baseline (c, d) can be found if preferred by pegging the two tapes at a and b instead of at A and B, and by then using lengths of 47'5" (14.46 m) and 39'0" (11.89 m). The net posts will be at n, n, and a 33'0" (10 m) singles net should be used.

When a combined doubles and singles court with a doubles net is used for singles, the net must be supported at the points n, n, to a height of 3 feet 6 inches (1.07 m) by means of two singles sticks, which shall be not more than 3 inches (7.5 cm) square or 3 inches (7.5 cm) in diameter. The centres of the singles sticks shall be 3 feet (.914 m) outside the singles court on each side.

To assist in the placing of these singles sticks it is desirable that the points n, n, should each be shown with a white dot when the court is marked.

Note: As a guide for international competitions, the recommended minimum distance between the baselines and the backstops should be 21 feet (6.40 m) and between the sidelines and the sidestops the recommended minimum distance should be 12 feet (3.66 m).

As a guide for recreational and Club play, the recommended minimum distance between the baselines and the backstops should be 18 feet (5.48 m) and between the sidelines and the sidestops the recommended minimum distance should be 10 feet (3.05 m).

As a guide, the recommended minimum top height to the ceiling should be 30 feet (9.14 m).

USTA Comment L.1: Tennis Court Layout

All courts should be laid out for singles and doubles play. The same lines—except for the sideline extensions for doubles play—are required for each.

Courts in the northern two-thirds of the United States should generally be laid out with the long axis north and south; it is advantageous, however, to orient the courts in the southern one-third of the country 15°-25° west of true (not magnetic) north in order to minimize the adverse effects of the afternoon winter sun.

Figure 1 indicates the exact dimensions of the lines as well as recommended side and back spacing. Note that the dimensions shown in the diagram are measurements to the outside edge of the lines. For regulation play, the space behind the baseline (between the baseline and fence) should not be less than 21 feet, for an overall dimension of 60' x 120'. For stadium courts, this perimeter spacing should be increased to allow space for Line Umpires without impeding the players. Net posts should be located with their centers three feet outside the doubles sideline.

Most courts are laid out with lines two inches (2") wide. Lines may be one inch (1") to two inches (2") wide excepting the center service line which must be two inches (2") wide and the baselines which may be up to four inches (4") wide.

For more detailed information on the subject, *Tennis Courts*, a book containing United States Tennis Association and American Sports Builders Association recommendations for the construction, maintenance, and equipment needs of a tennis court installation, can be obtained by calling 866-501-ASBA.

If you have a rules problem, send full details by email to officiating@usta.com, or by regular mail, enclosing a stamped self-addressed envelope, to USTA Tennis Rules and Regulations Committee, c/o Officials Department, 70 West Red Oak Lane, White Plains, NY 10604-3602.

The
Code

PREFACE

When a serve hits a player's partner who is stationed at the net, is it a let, fault, or loss of point? Likewise, what is the ruling when a serve, before touching the ground, hits an opponent who is standing back of the baseline? The answers to these questions are obvious to anyone who knows the fundamentals of tennis, but it is surprising the number of players who don't know these fundamentals. All players have a responsibility to be familiar with the basic rules and customs of tennis. Further, it can be distressing when a player makes a decision in accordance with a rule and the opponent protests with the remark: "Well, I never heard of that rule before!" Ignorance of the rules constitutes a delinquency on the part of a player and often spoils an otherwise good match.

What is written here constitutes the essentials of The Code, a summary of procedures and unwritten rules that custom and tradition dictate all players should follow. No system of rules will cover every specific problem or situation that may arise. If players of goodwill follow the principles of The Code, they should always be able to reach an agreement, while at the same time making tennis more fun and a better game for all. The principles set forth in The Code shall apply in cases not specifically covered by the ITF Rules of Tennis or the USTA Regulations.

Before reading this, the following question may come to mind: Since there is a book that contains all the rules of tennis, is there a need for The Code? Isn't it sufficient to know and understand all the rules? There are a number of things not specifically set forth in the rules that are covered by custom and tradition only. For example, if there is doubt on a line call, the opponent gets the benefit of the doubt. This result cannot be found in the rules. Further, custom dictates the standard procedures that players will use in reaching decisions. These are the reasons a code is needed.

—Col. Nick Powel

Note: The Code is not part of the official ITF Rules of Tennis. Players shall follow The Code in all unofficiated matches. Many of the principles also apply when officials are present. This edition of The Code is an adaptation of the original, which was written by Colonel Nicolas E. Powel.

PRINCIPLES

1. Courtesy is expected. Tennis is a game that requires cooperation and courtesy from all participants. The game of tennis is more fun when an opponent's good shots are praised. It is not so much fun when:

- Loud postmortems are conducted after points;

- Complaints are made about shots like lobs or drop shots;

- Weak opponents are embarrassed by a player's being overly gracious or condescending;

- Tempers are lost, vile language is used, rackets are thrown, or balls are slammed in anger; or

- Sulking occurs when losing.

2. Points played in good faith are counted. All points played in good faith stand. For example, if after losing a point, a player discovers that the net was four inches too high, the point stands. If a point is played from the wrong court, there is no replay. If during a point, a player realizes that a mistake was made at the beginning (for example, service from the wrong court), the player shall continue playing the point. Corrective action may be taken only after a point has been completed.

Shaking hands at the end of a match is an acknowledgment by the players that the match is over.

WARM-UP

3. Warm-up is not practice. A player should provide the opponent a 5-minute warm-up (ten minutes if there are no ballpersons). If a player refuses to warm up the opponent, the player forfeits the right to a warm-up. Some players confuse warm-up and practice. Each player should make a special effort to hit shots directly to the opponent. (If partners want to warm each other up while their opponents are warming up, they may do so.)

4. Warm-up serves and returns are taken before first serve of match. A player should take all warm-up serves before the first serve of a match. A player who returns serves should return them at a moderate pace in a manner that does not disrupt the server.

MAKING CALLS

5. Player makes calls on own side of net. A player calls all shots landing on, or aimed at, the player's side of the net.

6. Opponent gets benefit of doubt. When a match is played without officials, the players are responsible for making decisions, particularly for line calls. There is a subtle difference between player decisions and those of an on-court official. An official impartially resolves a problem involving a call, whereas a player is guided by the unwritten rule that any doubt must be resolved in favor of an opponent. A player in attempting to be scrupulously honest on line calls frequently will keep a ball in play that might have been out or that the player discovers too late was out. Even so, the game is much better played this way.

7. Ball touching any part of line is good. If any part of a ball touches a line, the ball is good. A ball 99% out is still 100% good. A player shall not call a ball out unless the player clearly sees space between where the ball hits and a line.

8. Ball that cannot be called out is good. Any ball that cannot be called out is considered to be good. A player may not claim a let on the basis of not seeing a ball. One of tennis' most infuriating moments occurs after a long hard rally when a player makes a clean placement and an opponent says: "I'm not sure if it was good or out. Let's play a let." Remember, it is each player's responsibility to call all balls landing on, or aimed at, the player's side of the net. If a ball cannot be called out with certainty, it is good. When a player says an opponent's shot was really out but offers to replay the point to give the opponent a break, it seems clear that the player actually doubted that the ball was out.

9. Either partner may make calls in doubles. Although either doubles partner may make a call, the call of a player looking down a line is much more likely to be accurate than that of a player looking across a line.

10. All points are treated the same regardless of their importance. All points in a match should be treated the same. There is no justification for considering a match point differently from a first point.

11. Requesting opponent's help. When an opponent's opinion is requested and the opponent gives a positive opinion, it must be accepted. If neither player has an opinion, the ball is considered good. Aid from an opponent is available only on a call that ends a point.

12. Out calls reversed. A player who calls a ball out shall reverse the call if the player becomes uncertain or realizes that the ball was good. The point goes to the opponent and is not replayed. However, when a receiver reverses a fault call on a serve that hit the net, the server is entitled to two serves.

13. Player calls own shots out. With the exception of the first serve, a player should call out the player's own shots if the player clearly sees the ball out regardless of whether requested to do so by an opponent. The prime objective in making calls is accuracy. All players should cooperate to attain this objective.

14. Partners' disagreement on calls. If one partner calls the ball out and the other partner sees the ball good, they shall call it good. It is more important to give opponents the benefit of the doubt than to avoid possibly hurting a partner's feelings. The tactful way to achieve the desired result is to tell a partner quietly of the mistake and then let the partner concede the point. If a call is changed from out to good, the principles of Code § 12 apply.

15. Audible or visible calls. No matter how obvious it is to a player that an opponent's ball is out, the opponent is entitled to a prompt audible or visible out call.

16. Spectators never make calls. A player shall not enlist the aid of a spectator in making a call. No spectator has a part in a match.

17. Prompt calls eliminate two chance option. A player shall make all calls promptly after a ball has hit the court. A call shall be made either before the player's return shot has gone out of play or before an opponent has had an opportunity to play the return shot.

Prompt calls will quickly eliminate the "two chances to win the point" option that some players practice. To illustrate, a player is advancing to the net for an easy put away and sees a ball from an adjoining court rolling toward the court. The player continues to advance and hits the shot, only to have the supposed easy put away fly over the baseline. The player then claims a let. The claim is not valid because the player forfeited the right to call a let by choosing instead to play the ball. The player took a chance to win or lose and is not entitled to a second chance.

18. Let called when ball rolls on court. When a ball from an adjacent court enters the playing area, any player on the court affected may call a let as soon as the player becomes aware of the ball. The player loses the right to call a let if the player unreasonably delays in making the call.

19. Touches, hitting ball before it crosses net, invasion of opponent's court, double hits, and double bounces. A player shall promptly acknowledge when:

- A ball in play touches the player;
- The player touches the net or opponent's court while a ball is in play;
- The player hits a ball before it crosses the net;
- The player deliberately carries or double hits a ball; or
- A ball bounces more than once in the player's court.

The opponent is not entitled to make these calls.

20. Balls hit through net or into ground. A player makes the ruling on a ball that the player's opponent hits:

- Through the net; or
- Into the ground before it goes over the net.

21. Making calls on clay courts. If any part of a ball mark touches a line on a clay court, the ball shall be called good. If only part of the mark on a court can be seen, this means that the missing part is on a line or tape. A player should take a careful second look at any point-ending placement that is close to a line on a clay court. Occasionally a ball will strike the tape, jump, and then leave a full mark behind the line. This does not mean that a player is required to show an opponent the mark. The opponent shall not pass the net to inspect a mark. If a player hears the sound of a ball striking the tape and sees a clean spot on the tape near the mark, the player should give the point to the opponent.

SERVING

22. Server's request for third ball. When a server requests three balls, the receiver shall comply when the third ball is readily available. Distant balls shall be retrieved at the end of a game.

23. Foot faults. The receiver or receiver's partner may call foot faults only after the server has been warned at least once and the request for an official has failed. This call should be made only when the receiver or receiver's partner is absolutely certain and the foot faulting is so flagrant as to be clearly perceptible from the receiver's side. The plea that a server should not be penalized because the server only touched the line and did not rush the net is not acceptable. Habitual foot faulting, whether intentional or careless, is just as surely cheating as is making a deliberate bad line call.

24. Service calls in doubles. In doubles the receiver's partner should call the service line, and the receiver should call the sideline and the center service line. Nonetheless, either partner may call a ball that either clearly sees.

25. Service calls by serving team. Neither the server nor server's partner shall make a fault call on the first service even if they think it is out because the receiver may be giving the server the benefit of the doubt. There is one exception. If the receiver plays a first service that is a fault and does not put the return in play, the server or server's partner may make the fault call. The server and the server's partner shall call out any second serve that either clearly sees out.

26. Service let calls. Any player may call a service let. The call shall be made before the return of serve goes out of play or is hit by the server or the server's partner. If the serve is an apparent or near ace, any let shall be called promptly.

27. Obvious faults. A player shall not put into play or hit over the net an obvious fault. To do so constitutes rudeness and may even be a form of gamesmanship. On the other hand, if a player does not call a serve a fault and gives the opponent the benefit of a close call, the server is not entitled to replay the point.

28. Receiver readiness. The receiver shall play to the reasonable pace of the server. The receiver should make no effort to return a serve when the receiver is not ready. If a player attempts to return a serve (even if it is a "quick" serve), then the receiver (or receiving team) is presumed to be ready.

29. Delays during service. When the server's second service motion is interrupted by a ball coming onto the court, the server is entitled to two serves. When there is a delay between the first and second serves:

- The server gets one serve if the server was the cause of the delay;
- The server gets two serves if the delay was caused by the receiver or if there was outside interference.

The time it takes to clear a ball that comes onto the court between the first and second serves is not considered sufficient time to warrant the server receiving two serves unless this time is so prolonged as to constitute an interruption. The receiver is the judge of whether the delay is sufficiently prolonged to justify giving the server two serves.

SCORING

30. Server announces score. The server shall announce the game score before the first point of a game and the point score before each subsequent point of the game.

31. Disputes. Disputes over the score shall be resolved by using one of the following methods, which are listed in the order of preference:

- Count all points and games agreed upon by the players and replay only disputed points or games;
- Play from a score mutually agreeable to all players;
- Spin a racket or toss a coin.

HINDRANCE ISSUES

32. Talking during point. A player shall not talk while a ball is moving toward an opponent's side of the court. If a player's talking interferes with an opponent's ability to play a ball, the player loses the point. For example, if a doubles player hits a weak lob and loudly yells at the player's partner to get back and if the shout is loud enough to distract an opponent, then the opponent may claim the point based on a deliberate hindrance. If the opponent chooses to hit the lob and misses it, the opponent loses the point because the opponent did not make a timely claim of hindrance.

33. Body movement. A player may feint with the body while a ball is in play. A player may change position at any time, including while the server is tossing a ball. Any other movement or any sound that is made solely to distract an opponent, including, but not limited to, waving arms or racket or stamping feet, is not allowed.

34. Let due to unintentional hindrance. A player who is hindered by an opponent's unintentional act or by something else outside the player's control is entitled to a let only if the player could have made the shot had the player not been hindered. A let is not authorized for a hindrance caused by something within a player's control. For example, a request for a let because a player tripped over the player's own hat should be denied.

35. Grunting. A player should avoid grunting and making other loud noises. Grunting and other loud noises may bother not only opponents but also players on adjacent courts. In an extreme case, an opponent or a player on an adjacent court may seek the assistance of the Referee or a Roving Umpire. The Referee or the Roving Umpire may treat grunting and the making of loud noises as hindrances. Depending upon the circumstance, this could result in a let or loss of point.

36. Injury caused by player. When a player accidentally injures an opponent, the opponent suffers the consequences. Consider the situation where the server's racket accidentally strikes the receiver and incapacitates the receiver. The receiver is unable to resume play within the time limit. Even though the server caused the injury, the server wins the match by retirement.

On the other hand, when a player deliberately injures an opponent and affects the opponent's ability to play, then the opponent wins the match by default. Hitting a ball or throwing a racket in anger is considered a deliberate act.

WHEN TO CONTACT OFFICIAL

37. Withdrawing from match or tournament. A player shall not enter a tournament and then withdraw when the player discovers that tough opponents have also entered. A player may withdraw from a match or tournament only because of injury, illness, or personal circumstance. A player who cannot play a match shall notify the Referee at once so that the opponent may be saved a trip.

38. Stalling. A player who encounters a problem with stalling should contact an official. The following actions constitute stalling:

- Warming up longer than the allotted time;
- Playing at about one-third a player's normal pace;
- Taking more than 90 seconds on the odd-game changeover or more than 2 minutes on the set break.
- Taking longer than the time authorized during a rest period;
- Starting a discussion or argument in order to rest;
- Clearing a missed first service that doesn't need to be cleared; or
- Excessive bouncing of a ball before any serve.

Stalling is subject to penalty under the Point Penalty System.

39. Requesting officials during play. While normally a player may not leave the playing area, the player may contact the Referee or a Roving Umpire to request assistance. Some reasons for contacting the Referee or a Roving Umpire include:

- Stalling;
- Flagrant foot faults;
- A medical or bleeding timeout;
- A scoring dispute; or
- A pattern of bad calls.

A player may refuse to play until an official responds.

BALL ISSUES

40. Retrieving stray balls. Each player is responsible for removing stray balls and other objects from the player's end of the court. Whenever a ball is not in play, a player must honor an opponent's request to remove a ball from the court or from an area outside the court that is reasonably close to the lines. A player shall not go behind an adjacent court to retrieve a ball or ask a player on an adjacent court to return a ball while a point is in play. When a player returns a ball from an adjacent court, the player shall wait until the point is over on the court where the ball is being returned and then return it directly to one of the players, preferably the server.

41. Catching a ball. If a player catches a ball before it bounces, the player loses the point regardless of where the player is standing.

42. New balls for third set. When a tournament specifies new balls for a third set, new balls shall be used unless all players agree otherwise.

MISCELLANEOUS

43. Clothing and equipment malfunction. If clothing or equipment, other than a racket, becomes unusable through circumstances outside the control of a player, play may be suspended for a reasonable period. A player may leave the court after a point is over to correct the problem. If a racket or string is broken, a player may leave the court to get a replacement, but the player is subject to code violations under the Point Penalty System.

44. Placement of towels. Towels are to be placed on the ground outside the net post or at the back fence. Clothing or towels should never be placed on a net.

NOTES

NOTES